LITTLE CITIZENS

WE TREAT OTHERS WELL

THERESA EMMINIZER

PowerKiDS press

Published in 2023 by The Rosen Publishing Group, Inc.
2544 Clinton St, Buffalo, NY 14224

First Edition

Editor: Theresa Emminizer
Book Design: Rachel Rising

Photo Credits: Cover, p. 1 Jacob Lund/Shutterstock.com; pp. 4, 6, 8, 10, 12, 14, 16, 18, 20 somen/Shutterstock.com; p. 5 Serhii Bobyk/Shutterstock.com; p. 7 Roman Samborskyi/Shutterstock.com; pp. 9, 15 LightField Studios/Shutterstock.com; pp. 11, 13 YAKOBCHUK VIACHESLAV/Shutterstock.com; pp. 17, 19 Monkey Business Images/Shutterstock.com; p. 21 Sergey Novikov/Shutterstock.com.

Library of Congress Cataloging-in-Publication Data
Names: Emminizer, Theresa.
Title: We Treat Others Well / Theresa Emminizer.
Description: New York : Powerkids Press, 2023. | Series: Little Citizens | Includes glossary and index.
Identifiers: ISBN 9781538389300 (pbk.) | ISBN 9781538389324 (library bound) | ISBN 9781538389331 (ebook)
Subjects: LCSH: Citizen participation–Juvenile literature.| Conduct of Life–Juvenile literature. | Kindess–Juvenile literature.
Classification: LCC 1533.K5 E46 2023 | DDC 177/.7083/4 –dc23

Manufactured in the United States of America

CPSIA Compliance Information: Batch #CWPK23. For Further Information contact Rosen Publishing at 1-800-237-9932.

CONTENTS

Be a Good Citizen

You belong to a community. You're a member of your country. You're a **citizen**! Citizens have **rights**. We also have **responsibilities**. We need to think about how our actions make a difference to others. Good citizens treat others well.

All Different, All the Same

Our community is made up of all kinds of people. We may be different ages. We may have different skin colors. We may be different sizes and shapes. Though we're all different, we all have feelings. And our feelings matter.

Show Respect

Every person is **worthy** of kindness and respect. Respect is a feeling of understanding and caring about someone's wishes and well-being. We can show respect to others even if they aren't our friends. Being polite and listening well are great ways to start!

Kindness in Action

Every day at lunchtime, Tori sits with a big group of her friends. They eat and talk. It's Tori's favorite part of the day! But Tori notices something. Her classmate Ben always sits all by himself. Ben doesn't have any friends.

Tori wonders if Ben is lonely. She knows she would be! Tori asks Ben to sit at her table. At first, Ben seems nervous. But soon he looks happy. Tori is happy too. It feels good to help her classmate!

Be Inclusive

Being excluded, or left out, can hurt our feelings. One of the best ways we can treat others well is by being inclusive! That means inviting others to take part in things. There's room for everybody when we play and share.

Kindness in Action

Shane doesn't like talking in front of others. When he speaks, he has a hard time getting the words out. Especially when he's nervous. Shane feels **embarrassed** about being different. He worries that the other kids will make fun of him.

One day, Shane is asked to read aloud in class. Shane's voice shakes. Ted, Shane's classmate, wants to help. He wants Shane to feel better. When Shane stops reading, Ted claps for him. The other kids start clapping too! Shane smiles.

Sight words
live out people
who work
5. white
6. bike
7. dime
8. hide
9. ice
10. kite

The Golden Rule

There are so many ways to practice kindness every day. You've probably heard of the golden rule: treat others as you would have them treat you. Follow this rule to help make your community a better, kinder place for everybody.

GLOSSARY

citizen: One who lives in a country legally and has certain rights.

embarrassed: Feeling uncomfortable or nervous.

responsibility: Something a person is in charge of.

right: Something someone is allowed to have, get, or do by law.

worthy: Having value.

FOR MORE INFORMATION

BOOKS

Morlock, Rachael. *I Am Kind Online*. New York, NY: PowerKids Press, 2020.

Turner, Joshua. *What Is Respect?* New York, NY: PowerKids Press, 2020.

WEBSITES

PBS Kids

pbskids.org/video/dots-spot/3017811961

Watch this fun video about what it means to be kind!

School of Kindness

schoolofkindness.org/random-acts-of-kindness-for-kids

Read these ideas for practicing kindness.

Publisher's note to educators and parents: Our editors have carefully reviewed these websites to ensure that they are suitable for students. Many websites change frequently, however, and we cannot guarantee that a site's future contents will continue to meet our high standards of quality and educational value. Be advised that students should be closely supervised whenever they access the internet.

INDEX